# Treasures
# From
# Heaven

Cynthia Rose Ingram

# Treasures from Heaven

# Dedication

I dedicate this book to all who feel they are in a desert experience, or those who have felt like they have been dumped in the desert.

There may be times when we all have these feelings. I would encourage you to hang in there. We have a God who will never leave us or forsake us. He is always there to extend a hand. All we have to do is call upon His Name, and believe that He will answer. He will bring us through the dry, parched land and refresh us with His Word and presence.

Most of all, I dedicate this to my children, Christopher and Patricia, and my grandsons, Justin and Ryan, who are to me, more precious than any gem on earth.

May you be blessed as you read each poem.

Cynthia Rose Ingram

# Acknowledgements

I would like to take the time to thank the following special people who have been such an encouragement to me. They have pressed me onward to write this book.

Janice Wilson, I first met her in Israel while on a tour there. You are a God given angel who has walked with me through many a storm. You have a tremendous gift of discernment and intimate walk with the Lord. You truly are a Woman of God whom I admire greatly.

Kay Huffman, thank you for dropping sparkles of gems and pearls in my life by always encouraging me onward. You have shown me how to worship through dance, and how to gather the "jewels" from heaven. You are a powerful intercessor and Worship Warrior for the Lord. I admire you for your Lion's roar of strength and courage through the battles.

Jane Dulla, some of the poems came through a word spoken by you. You were always there with an encouraging word to "go for it", and many a poem you were the first to review. Your friendship and support are greatly appreciated.

Paulette Luke, who is now dancing on the streets of gold with the Lord, her prayers and belief that I could do it, have been most inspiring to me.

I can't forget Dr. Comstock and Dr. Nakazato, who have encouraged me to write a poem in jest.

Most of all, I give the highest praise and thanksgiving to my Abba Father, Jeshua and the Ruach HaKodesh, who reveals to all those who have a hunger and thirst for intimacy with Him. Revelation comes through seeking Him diligently.

# Contents

# Pearls for the Bride ........................ 77

# Sapphires Glowing with the Father's Desire ..... 101

# Diamond Facets from the Heart

# A New Year's Prayer

As I begin the New Year,
Lord, my prayers please hear.
May this be a year of surprises,
As the morning sun arises.
With the clarion sound,
May miracles abound.
While healings mightily occur,
Enable men's spirits to stir.
Bring us to our knees;
Release the storehouse of heaven with Your keys.
Open our eyes each day,
To whatever You bring our way.
Open our ears to hear what the Spirit has to say.
May we be obedient every moment of the day.
Open our heart with Your love to receive;
Deepen our reins with faith to believe.
Each day as we grow older,
Make our witness bolder.
Meet us in Your secret place;
Fill us with Your mercy and grace.
The days are flying by so fast,
Let us not dwell on the past.
A soldier You've called us to be,
In Your name to conquer and set free.
Sharpen the iron upon our sword,
As we speak the Truth, You are Lord.
We're open now to hear Your Word,
And ready to move forward!

## Daily Prayer

Lord, I pray,
Help us today.
Give us a gentle heart,
Let that be our start.
To all the devious lies,
Open our eyes.
May the words of our mouth,
Profess what Truth is about.
May we respond to another's pain,
And not look to what we can gain.
May the work of our hands
Enable us to take our stands.
Lord, to You, the breath of our life,
We surrender our struggle and strife.
Cover us with Your shield;
To You alone, our life we yield.

# Work Prayer

Lord, I have to go to work today.
In Your presence I'd rather stay.
To remain forever true,
Keep me close to You.
My heart is so on fire;
You are my only desire!
Help me to remain pure,
Away from worldly lure.
A daily reading of Your Word,
Will help me to move forward.
Show me Your perfect way,
Leading me on this day,
Along the path of my destiny,
With You, toward Eternity.

# Wind of the Spirit

Wind of the Holy Spirit blow,
Help my spirit to grow.
Holy wind from the North,
Healing bring forth.
Holy wind from the South,
Spread Your glory about.
Holy wind from the West,
Help me be obedient in each test.
Holy wind from the East,
Prepare me for the Bridal feast.
Holy Spirit, as You rest in me,
Open my eyes to see,
The beauty that surrounds me,
And wonders that are coming to be.
Open my ears to hear,
The mysteries You hold dear.
Your grace and mercy to believe,
Open my hands to receive.
Open my mouth to say,
"Jesus is the only Truth and Way."
Help me to be bold,
And speak all that I'm told.
So that I'll not stray,
Guide me in Your way.
As the earth starts to groan and rumble,
Keep me pure and humble.
When devastation comes along,
Help me to stand strong.
As I hold onto the fringes of Your garment,
Clothe me in Your perfect armament;
Your righteousness as the breastplate,
Your shield for faith;
A girdle of Truth around the middle;

Feet shod with Truth, not a riddle.
Salvation as a helmet upon my head,
By Your Word, the sword, boldly led.
Here, I stand, as Your Warrior Bride,
Ready to saddle up and ride.
With the single eye like the dove,
I'll ride on Your wings of love.
Here I am Lord,
Bound to You in one accord.

## Rain from Heaven

When the rain falls from Heaven,
Let it wash away the leaven.
With a fine sprinkle, cleansing the earth,
From Heaven's fountain, it brings new birth.
Mercy flowing, washes away our fears,
Like a shower, these are Your precious tears.
Lord, please open our eyes,
To see Your coming in the skies.
Lord, I know Your coming is soon.
Will it be midnight or high noon?
Time is rushing by;
To You, it's a blink of the eye.
Lord, when I look up into the sky,
I look for Your appearance, as the clouds roll by.

# Peace Be Still

Do you hear the harps playing?
My dear, what are they saying?
"Peace be still!"; "Peace be still!"
Yes, Lord, I'll do Your will.
Make Your presence known to me,
So Your glory I will see.
Capture me in Your arms of love;
Sing to me, like the turtledove.
My eyes are teary,
My body is so weary.
Smelling of a Rose of Sharon fragrance,
How I long for Your presence.
You make a life complete;
Nothing is discreet.
You bring healing in Your wings.
Holy fire come, my body sings!
Purge me and cleanse me;
Set my body, soul and spirit free!

## Vessel of Love

Created from above,
Is a pure vessel of love.
A touch from the Master's hand
Chooses the vessel where it will land.
A vessel tried and true,
Many tend to misconstrue.
A heart that's ripped apart,
In Him, has a new start.
A heart humble and meek,
Is one whom the Lord will seek.
A heart that's laid upon the altar,
One in Him, will not falter.
In the world, it forfeits things,
To the altar, his life he brings.
A heart that's purged by fire,
Is the one that the Father and Son admire.
We surrender our hearts to You, Lord;
Bind us together in one accord.

## Whispers From Above

Do you hear the rustle of the leaves,
As the palm tree sways in the breeze?
"Come to Me, My love,"
He whispers from above.
"My love is pure
My love is sure
My love is real
Can you the fire feel?"
"Yes, Lord, I do!
To You I will remain true.
Lord, I love You so much.
I long for Your gentle touch."
"Of My love so true,
I will sing to you.
It will set you on fire,
And change your whole attire!"

# Writer's Prayer

Coming down from above,
Are whispers of the Father's love.
Each line of every verse,
Flows like honey, as we converse.
Your words are filled with might.
Words of love, such a delight!
Help me Lord, in obedience to write,
Prayerfully aware, to do it right.
Pondering every word that's deep,
Help me to remember, even while I'm asleep.
Coming from Your silver and gold mine,
How I savor each precious line.
You love us so much!
It's our heart You long to touch.
Lord, place Your pen in my hand,
With writers ink to take a stand!

## Ancient of Days

Oh Ancient of Days,
Let me walk in Your ways.
Like the Prophets of old,
Many have stories untold.
Breathe in me Your precious Word.
Let it go forth like the song of a bird.
As it penetrates a heart,
Let it pierce like a dart,
To bring revival
And for a soul, survival.
Use me as a vessel so pure,
Through Your love, many to lure,
To Your haven of rest,
Gathered close to Your chest.
Before time runs out,
Let them hear Your clarion shout.

## Heart on Fire

A heart on fire
Is Your desire.
It's a flame of passion,
In a fiery fashion,
Ascending to Your throne,
For You alone.
Seeking to dwell in Love's pure mansion,
Make me a flame, burning with compassion.
Set my heart aflame,
Seal it with the Father's claim.
With Him in Eternity,
May it forever be.

# Cheery Greeting

A cheery morning greeting to you;
May it be a fantastic day too!
On wings of Love, as you ride,
May every burden be cast aside.
With a morning drink of His Word, like sweet wine,
May you be enraptured with the Divine.
As you dance with prayer all through the day,
May you be enfolded in His arms, I pray!

## Prayer for America

America, America, I will pray for you,
You, who wave the red white and blue.
One Nation formed under God,
Lord, I pray, please stay Judgment's rod.
The stripes of white, a symbol of the pure,
I humbly pray, they will not become obscure.
The strips of deep red,
Is a symbol of the blood that was shed.
The blood cries out from all over the land;
Righteous in Christ, you must take a stand!
The stars arranged on the heavenly blue,
Remind us of what is true.
You are the only true God in the Universe,
Who longs so much with us to converse.
Rend our hearts and souls this day;
Have mercy upon America, I pray!

# Healing Waters

Abba Father, this I pray,
Send Your healing waters today.
Flowing from the head to the toes,
Let it bring perfect healing as it flows.
While You hung upon that rugged tree,
All pain and disease, You bore for me.
My head I humbly bow,
I accept Your healing now.
Thank You Lord, for all You've done,
I know the battle has been won.
I pray Shalom over all who read this,
And ask the Father to seal it with a kiss.

# Time

Time is going by so fast.
How long will time last?
Decisions are being made.
Plans are being laid.
Will we choose what's right?
Will it be to God's delight?
On our knees we must pray,
And in His presence continually stay.
Every moment of the day,
He will show us the way.

# Prophet of Old

Oh Prophet of old,
Why do you carry that heavy load?
Is it for the Nations?
Is it a sack full of oblations?
Where are you traveling to,
And what will you do?
May I follow you,
And carry a sack or two?
That I may not stray,
Show me the way.
I seek to follow you,
And see His glory too.
The road is so narrow and winding.
This load is heavy and binding.
It's such and arduous trek up the hill,
While the earth is so silently still.
I suddenly feel her pain under my feet.
The groaning and grumbling are ready to meet.
The mountains seem to tremble,
As if all creation is ready to re-assemble.
To reckon with man for his sin,
Is judgment about to begin?
The Nations are in such an uproar,
Tell me, dear Prophet, what's in store?
Will they come around,
Before the trumpet makes a sound?
Will they acknowledge the true King,
Before the judgment He will bring?
Up to the altar too,
Oh Prophet, I will follow you.
I will lay my sack upon the wood,
For in His Word, I have stood.
May the flames of the fire burn brightly,

And cleanse us from sins unsightly.
May a sweet fragrance arise,
And tears of repentance fill our eyes.
May revival come upon the land,
While near the altar we stand.
As a mantle to cover all,
May His grace and mercy fall.
When repentance rises over all the earth,
May all receive New Birth.

## Holy Spirit Come

Holy Spirit You're my desire
Fill me with Your consuming fire.
By being obedient and still,
Help me walk in Your will.
To compromise,
Close my eyes.
Your whispers to hear,
Open each ear.
Open my mouth,
Let Your words come out.
Here are my hands,
Let them do Your plans.
Burn through to my feet,
A flame of love to all I meet.
A holy temple unto You,
Fill me through and through.
Let nothing come my way,
That doesn't edify You today.
Flame of Love, burn within,
Purge me of all my sin.
Let my life grow brighter,
A flaming warrior, Your fighter.
Help me to see,
The destiny You've planned for me.
Help me to walk it out,
With Your clarion shout!

# As a Child

Lord, I come to You as a child,
So gentle, meek and mild.
Under Your Tallit wrap,
I want to sit in Your lap.
Please tell me stories of old.
I know there are many to be told.
Explain all the mysteries to me,
And open my eyes to see.
Show me the wonders that You created,
And all the Prophets that You led.
I'm in awe of what You have to say,
And how You came to save the day.
While Your perfect love enfolds me,
I can feel Your heart beating so free.
With my human frustrations,
You are so patient with my questions.
There's so much peace within Your arms,
No disturbance, not even one that alarms.
A peace that passes all understanding You say,
This is how it's to be every day.
The cares of the world don't matter much,
When focused on Heaven's touch.
Snuggled against Your chest for a nap,
I want to stay forever in Your lap.

# Thank You for This Day

I thank you for this time today.
I pray my heart with You to stay.
Whispers of love to You,
My spirit sends all day through.
No matter what comes my way,
I know You're in me to stay.
I believe You are my Savior and Lord.
I now put on faith's shield, and the Spirit's sword.
With the helmet of salvation upon my head,
By Your girdle of Truth I am led.
I place the shoes of peace upon my feet, and add Your vest;
A breastplate of righteousness upon my chest.
I stand boldly as Your warrior of worship,
Ready for You to send on the assigned trip.
By being crucified upon that tree,
Thank You Lord, for all You've done for me.

# Emeralds of Encouragement

# Be Encouraged

To find out where we belong,
We must stand and be strong.
Nothing will be a catastrophe,
All good things will flow naturally.
So, let us lift our heads up high,
And turn our face to the sky.
We'll put a smile upon our face,
And carry on in this earthly place.
All good things come to those who wait.
God's timing is never late!
Justice will prevail;
God will never let us fail.
This is just a little word or two,
To help carry us right on through!

# A Broken Heart

A broken heart can be mended,
Just position yourself on knees bended.
A wounded heart has much pain,
From the unforgiveness it tries to contain.
But, who can bear a pierced heart,
From the iniquity that penetrates like a dart?
Jesus bore our pain and sin,
That Eternal life we may enter in.
All He asks is for us to believe,
And open our hearts to receive.

# Hope

When you're at the end of your rope,
Beloved, there is always hope.
The Lord's hand is extended to you.
His love will carry you through.
He promises to never leave or forsake us.
Why do we not trust, but make a big fuss?
Trust in Him to carry you through.
He will refresh you as the morning dew.
He will carry you on His wings.
A peace that passes all understanding He brings.
Surrounded by the fragrance of a precious flower,
He will shelter you in His strong tower.
Believe He is there.
He will carry your care.
Shalom in front of you, and beside you;
Shalom in back of you,
And, most of all, inside you!

## Tree of Life

Standing under the Tree of Life,
I feel no pain or strife.
The healing leaves rustle above me,
And my eyes open to see,
Miracles flowing all around,
As they gently flow to the ground.
They leave a presence of glory,
As I enter into His story.
His presence is so real,
His gentleness and love I feel.
The fragrance of the tree,
Totally surrounds me.
Like a fragrance of roses, oh so sweet,
It permeates slowly down to my feet.
How I love to sit with Him,
Where the light is never dim.
To hear His gentle voice,
Will always be my choice.
Some day in Heaven above,
I'll be surrounded by His love.
With a love flowing over my brim,
I will sing and dance for Him.
I'll twirl
And whirl,
Raising a banner up high,
It will float all over the sky.
Forever in Eternity
With Him we'll be!

# Cherries

Cherries, cherries all around,
Falling gently to the ground.
Why do you think
The blossoms are so pink?
"May I have a dance or two?
I long to romance you!
The flowering season is so short,
But not the ones around My court.
As petals fall to the ground,
Death to self is all around.
The fruit then must mature,
Through rain and wind it must endure.
The touch of the Son will ripen the cherry.
In fullness of time, all will be merry!
The heavens resound with My song,
Come My Bride and dance along.
Cherries, cherries all around,
Step lightly on the ground.
Mash the fruit to a pulp,
So you can savor every gulp.
The juice is so divine!
Come, drink of My heavenly wine!
Come, My Bride, to the heavenly table.
In My presence you'll always be stable.
Drink in celebration with Me,
My beautiful Bride, forever in Eternity!"

# Appreciation

You've done a great job today!
Remember, you're special in every way!
You deserve a star or two,
For all the hard work you do.
I appreciate you helping out.
You deserve a big shout!
Hip, Hip Hooray!
You shine today!
Your work day is now done,
So, enjoy your evening and have fun!
Be safe, as you head on home.
You're the star of this poem!

## Song of the Cardinal

Says the Cardinal from above,
I'll sing a song to you my love.
You are precious in His sight,
And such a delight!
I love to sing to you.
I know that you enjoy it too.
So, listen to my song today.
It will guide you on your way!

## A Precious Rose for You

As grace with mercy flows,
He sends to you a precious rose.
The Lord wants you to know,
He loves you so!
Flowing down from your head to your feet,
The fragrance is, oh so sweet.
The petals are soft and velvet to touch;
His tender love brings so much!
The aroma gently enfolds you,
Like the freshness of morning dew.
Shades of pink and shades of red,
Thank Him for the blood He shed.
The green stem, a symbol of Eternity,
Forever with Him we will be!

## The Father's Comfort

When your world seems like it's caving in,
Look to your Father in Heaven.
His arms are opened wide.
He will gently enfold you inside.
He's there to comfort you.
He understands what you're going through.
He will wipe away your tears,
And allay all your fears.
Just lean on His chest,
He will give you perfect rest.
Resonating with a heavenly sound,
His light will shine all around.
He will whisper of His love to you,
It'll make your heart skip a beat or two.
Joy will return to you,
With an overflowing in all you say and do.
This He wants you to know;
So, give Him complete control.

## Roses for Trials

A bouquet of roses coming to you,
For all the trials you go through.
May each rose bloom every day
With a fragrance that will stay.
While savoring the smell of a rose,
A thorn may prick a finger or a nose.
Sending thorns from the head to the toes,
Every trial is like that rose.
In the end, love and beauty will prevail;
All intended evil will fail.
May this encourage you this day,
As you walk along life's pathway.
Remember,
You are precious and loved!

# Ungrateful

Sometimes a day goes by
And you don't even hear a "Hi."
It can be an unthankful job,
And you just want to sob.
What has happened to the human race,
When they can't even say "thanks" to your face?
You try your best to make things go smooth,
Yet, there are those who scrutinize every move.
Because they don't like your choice,
They raise their voice.
You try to lend a helping hand,
They fuss like an out of tune band.
What can one do?
Just follow what is true.
We all run a different race,
And have our own special place.
Then one day, someone shows they care,
With a smile or compliment about your hair.
Forgiveness cancels all injustice done.
Once more, the challenge in life has begun!

# The Second Hand Rose

A mere spectacle for all to see,
A second hand rose I have felt to be.
Petals all so wilted,
Like a wife who's been jilted.
Leaves and stems so brown,
Like a statue who has lost a crown.
The faint, sweet scent has remained,
Once a beauty in life, now drained.
Lord, only You can restore a life,
And make her Your beautiful wife.
With a beautiful radiance and so demure,
She's clothed in petals so pristine and pure.
Emerald leaves to embrace her beauty;
Bound to worship is her duty.
Stems to hold her up high,
They never again will sag or sigh.
Her fragrance fills the air.
All who pass, stop and stare.
A beauty You have created.
Your love is never belated.
Especially in moments of despair,
Your love is always there.
Bringing her into a sweet repose,
You gently cradle Your sweet rose.

## Hugs are Precious

Do you feel the strings of your heart tug?
Maybe you need a hug.
Everyone needs a hug now and then.
One never knows just when.
Soon someone passes by,
With a caring voice says, "Hi!"
You feel like you're about to cry,
Then arms reach out as if to touch the sky.
A warm embrace enfolds you,
While caring love pours through.
"Thank you," are the words you say.
"I sure needed that hug today!"

## People Hear

Many people are hurting so bad.
They are so hungry and sad.
Jesus, You are the Way, Truth and Light!
The Nations must turn and give up their flight.
Waiting for you to come with a stride,
He is standing there with His arms open wide.
So that with Him we might sup,
On the cross His life He gave up.
Time is running out,
Do you hear the clarion shout?
His pace is a running.
For His Bride He is coming!
Let Him purify your heart.
That's where it all must start.
He will make it like gold,
Never for a price to be sold!
Satan will try to tear you apart,
But, Jesus holds in His palm, your heart.
Come, come to Him.
Turn away from all your sin!
From the deception, by which the world is led,
He'll carry you through the days ahead.
"Help the people to understand.
There is a far better land.
You are a special Ambassador of Mine,
You are only here for a short time."

## Butterfly Blessings

Butterfly blessings are coming this day,
Fluttering down in a special way!
May they bring words of cheer,
While Angels whisper in your ear.
Perfected by each trial with strife,
You are a special flower in the garden of life.
Planted firmly on the earth in sod,
You are watered with the love of God.
Open up your blossoms wide,
And let His love pour inside.

# A Pearl

Opalescent, by far,
A pearl you are.
A diamond in the rough,
Proven in Him to be tough.
A ruby on fire,
For Him is the desire.
A sapphire in radiant blue,
To Him remain true.
An emerald so glowing,
His righteousness He's bestowing.
All the gems can't compare,
To the love He has to share.

# Costly Rubies of Love

# Messiah Born

On a dark and silent night,
Into the world came a bright light.
Wise men saw the light from afar.
They followed the light of the star.
While shepherds watched their flocks that night,
They stood in awe at the star so bright.
As the light shone upon a manger,
A new born child began to stir.
"All honor and glory to the new born King,"
The heavenly choir began to sing.
On bended knees the Wise men fell.
"Who is this new born babe, pray tell?"
At God's appointed time,
His Son was born from David's line.
A Messiah born to save mankind from sin,
And restore Heaven's Covenant with Him.
May the true meaning of His birth fill your heart,
With a love for Messiah, that will never depart!

## The Wise Men

The Wise Men sought Him,
They came from a far,
To a little town in Bethlehem,
Following the Star!
They found Him, a babe in the manger.
They knelt to worship and adore.
The new born King, a stranger
Whose life became so much more!
Wise men still seek Him
For Truth must be found.
Their light, no longer dim,
Will shine with His peace all around.

## The Man from Galilee

Oh Man from Galilee,
How I love to worship Thee!
With my hands raised up high,
I feel I could span the sky!
My mouth is opened wide,
Proclaiming Your love in my stride!
Oh Man from Galilee,
Let Your glory flow free,
So that the whole world would see,
Your love as it was meant to be.
Your light shines so bright,
As I proclaim You with all my might.
I'm carried on Your wings of love,
Clothed in Your glory from above!
Oh Man from Galilee,
I'm so in love with Thee!

# A Walk along the Galilee

Walking by the Sea of Galilee,
Peter and Andrew He did see.
"I will make you fishers of men,
Who will turn to Me from their sin."
James and John were next in line,
They came to taste the Heavenly wine.
Philip and Bartholomew were next to come,
To follow the heartbeat of heaven's drum.
Thomas and Matthew joined the troop,
Then James and Thaddeus entered the group.
Simon came and wouldn't go past.
Then along came Judas, who was the last.
To answer the Master's call,
Twelve disciples came in all.
Eleven remained faithful to Him,
Except the one who betrayed Him on a whim.
Eleven roses in a bouquet,
One is absent because of betray.
For the blood that He shed,
The edges are trimmed in red.
Adding the color of pink to blend,
It stands for His healing power to mend.
Entering into His glory stream,
There's a subtle touch of cream.
Cupped in His mercy unseen,
Each rose is cradled in green.
The stems standing so straight,
Signifying, we enter only through His gate.
His promise is wrapped with a bow.
One day in the Rapture we will go!

# Before Pilate

As He stood before Pilate,
He was silent.
To a King, who was humbled so low,
Every whiplash became a heavy blow.
They placed a garment of red,
Over His body, as He bled.
While He stood silently in place,
They laughed and jeered in His face.
A crown of thorns was placed upon His head.
Like a lamb to slaughter, He was led.
Stumbling along Calvary's road,
The weight of our sin was His load.
As the accusers cheered on,
Jeshua knew victory would soon be won.
As they threw the dice,
He was paying our price.
At the foot of the cross, they bet for His garment.
Suddenly, all became silent.

## Calvary's Road

Walking down the Calvary road,
Upon my back is a heavy load.
In a distance three crosses I see.
I wonder in my heart, what that could be.
They say a King was born near here.
Is His presence near?
I feel the earth suddenly quake.
My knees begin to shimmer and shake.
The load becomes heavy in my sack.
The tears in my eyes, I can't hold back.
Three men on the crosses I now see,
One gazes so intently upon me.
One is angry and shouting so loud,
Yelling curses at the crowd.
One said, "Lord, remember me."
He said, "In Paradise today you'll be."
His gaze upon me becomes so long.
The pain in my heart is so strong.
I see a crown of thorns upon His head.
Is this the King to whom I'm led?
With His last breath, I hear Him call.
Unable to stand, upon my knees I fall.
A drop of blood falls upon my head.
This is the King, to whom I was led.

## Kneeling Under the Cross

Under the cross I kneel,
His presence I strongly feel.
While I gaze upon His hands,
Another drop of blood upon me lands.
With a gentle touch,
These hands did so much.
Many were healed,
Demons were revealed,
As the crowds upon Him pressed,
Many were blessed.
The nails look rusty and old,
The pounding was brutal, I'm told.
I can feel His hand extended to me.
Saying, while gasping, "You now are free."
My heart skips another beat,
As I now look upon His feet.
While the soldiers gather all around,
His blood is pouring to the ground.
One pierces Him with a sharp rod.
Another says, "This truly is the Son of God."
The water and blood pour forth from His side.
Why do the soldiers continue to chide?
I feel a deep pain in my heart.
From the cross I must not part.
Lord, forgive me for the wrong I've done.
Thank You for the victory You've won.
A daily dying to self, being my loss,
Keep my eyes focused on Your work on the cross.
As I gaze upon You on the cross above,
I'm reminded of Your endless love.

## Seven Ways the Lord Bled

With tearful eyes, covered with a haze,
Upon a wooden cross I gaze.
What happened here so many years ago?
The depth, Lord, I want to know.
I heard it said,
There are seven ways Jeshua bled.
Drops of blood fell from His brow, a test of will,
In the garden while the night was still.
As He struggled with emotions, evil came to harass.
He cried to the Father three times, that the cup would pass.
Beads of bloody perspiration fell to the ground.
He surrendered His will; now He was Calvary bound.
They tore the flesh from His back.
With a cat-o-nine tail, they spared no slack.
While the flesh from His body was peeled,
By His stripes we were healed.
He was bruised for our iniquities and sin.
His blood shed that heaven we could enter in.
A symbol of authority, where Adam failed,
His hands were bound, and nailed.
His blood poured forth upon the ground,
Authority in Him has rebound.
The nails were pound into His feet.
Symbolize dominion, where heaven and earth meet.
A sword, pierced His forgiving heart,
To fill us with joy, that would never depart.
The blood shed from the crown upon His head,
Dealt with poverty and lack; they're now dead.
I ponder the love that poured forth from the cross,
And consider my life to be a loss.
For the only truth to remain,
Is Eternal life for me to gain.
Forgiveness for my sin,

Starts with a life surrendered to Him.
For hardened hearts to awake,
One drop of His blood is all it would take.
The joy to know Him and the power of His suffering,
Enters us into Eternal life with our King!

# Ponder

I ponder the crown upon His head.
Multiple bruises and cuts remain where He bled.
Oh, the pain He must have felt,
While with my sin He dwelt and dealt.
The crown, made from wood,
Came from the earth where He stood.
The weight of the crown penetrated His skin,
His blood became an exchange for my sin.
The tears I can't hold back.
In me there is so much lack.
I hear His gentle voice say,
"Look to Me, I am the Way.
The pain I bore for you,
When I shed My blood too.
I did it out of love for you,
So you can have a life anew.
Rise up in the victory I have won.
My precious warrior, you must carry on!
A battle is raging.
The end time is staging.
You must be strong.
By My side you belong.
You are a warrior so fair,
So let go of every care.
For you are upon this earth as a lease,
Now, enter into My peace.
Soon on My white horse I'll come.
Listen for the sound of the distant drum.
Heaven's trumpet will blast,
As I come for My Bride at last.
I'll gather My army with Me,
To march and destroy the enemy."
All creation will bow to the King.

The Angels will join with the Bride to sing.
"Glory and honor be unto The Ancient of Days."
All mankind will stand or fall under His gaze.
No longer will mankind wink and nod,
They will know this is truly, the Son of God!

## Man of Pain

My dear, sweet Man of pain,
I'm so glad You came.
You bore my pain,
To give me Your name.
Risen to show us a tomorrow,
You truly are a Man of sorrow.
For my broken heart,
You gave me Your promise to never part.
For the pain in my head,
By Your Spirit, I must be led.
For the pain in my soul,
You died to make me whole.
For my frazzled emotions,
Myrrh and frankincense are soothing potions.
You're the only one, who can make me whole,
And restore what the enemy stole.
All my pains and sorrows,
From the yesterdays, todays and tomorrows,
I now give them all to You,
For I know Your Word is true.
Truly, You are the victorious One!
Thank You Father, for sending Your Son!

## Sound of Your Voice

The sound of Your voice is like thunder.
It can throw creation asunder.
When the earth starts to quake,
And the mountains begin to shake,
It draws the attention of mankind,
To panic, or a prayer comes to mind.
At the sound of Your voice,
We must make a choice.
Will we be obedient to what You say,
Or will we continue on our own way?
To keep us from a tumble,
Sometimes it takes a rumble.
Obedience to You, is the best way to go.
It will keep us safe, and help us to spiritually grow.

## The Tomb Is Empty

On this Resurrection day, Lord,
To You our eyes are turned toward.
An Angel was sitting upon the tomb,
We pondered what took place in that room.
"Don't fear,
Jeshua is not here.
Just like He said,
He's risen from the dead."
The words pierce my heart.
An excitement begins to start.
I must go see.
Where can He be?
"Oh Sir, can you tell me where He is?
I was just told He lives."
As the man turned toward me,
He spoke, and I could see.
As I stepped forward,
It was my Lord!
He said to me,
"I must go to the Father you see.
When I return,
Hearts will burn,
Truth will be said,
I have risen from the dead.
Don't fear!
No longer into the tomb leer."
Jeshua now sits upon the throne.
We are not left alone.
For He has made a way,
And intercedes for us every day.
He came to set us free,
To be with Him forever, in Eternity!

# Hallelujah!

Jesus Christ has risen from the dead!
By His Spirit we now are led.
To unlock all His power and authority,
He has given us the Kingdom key.
We are to be a warrior people,
Not bound to hide inside a steeple.
Ready to travel to every Nation,
We are an over-comer generation.
With His sword in our hand,
We're ready to take a stand.
So that all Nations will have heard,
We are to spread His Word.
His Kingdom has come,
His sovereign will shall be done.
He is Lord of lords, and King of kings!
Salvation to all, He brings.
When we surrender our life at the cross,
We will suffer flesh and earthly loss.
When the things of this world fade away,
Secure in His arms we will stay.
A heart devoted to Him alone,
Freely enters His majestic throne.
Sons and daughters of the King,
Let the Halleleujahs ring!
Our Passover lamb is alive!
In His Word, we will thrive!

## Passover's Meaning

During this Holy season,
Let's remember the real reason.
It's not about a bunny,
Or ham with gravy that's runny,
Or baskets filled with candy,
Or colored eggs that look so dandy.
Listen, as the Angels shout.
This is what it's about!
To bear our sin and bring New Birth,
The Son of God came to earth.
On the cross He bore our sin,
That eternal life we may enter in.
He rose from the grave the third day.
He is alive to show us the way.
The chains of death were broken;
May our spirits be woken.
As it flows freely from above,
May we believe and feel His love.
Let us surrender our life to Him.
He will help us run the race to win!

## Boldly Enter

During this Passover time,
Let our hearts align
With the Father above,
Who sent His Son out of love.
Bound by sin from the fall,
Jeshua came to redeem us all.
He opened heaven's door,
And came to restore,
A relationship with the Father above,
Who loves with an unfailing love.
The throne we can boldly go near,
For Jeshua's blood washed away the fear.
It is through His blood we enter in,
His life laid down for our sin.
No greater love can be found!
Give Him your heart for peace to abound!

## The Cross

On the cross He died and bled,
To become our daily bread.
His blood was poured out for our sin,
That eternal life we may win.
So that our bodies would be healed,
His body was scourged and peeled.
Upon His head a crown was put in place,
One that ripped and tore into His face.
Oh, such love and sacrifice He gave;
Atonement for our sin, us to save.
Open your heart when you hear His call.
His love, mercy and grace upon you will fall.

# Pearls for the Bride

# A Bridal Call

It's time for autumn leaves to fall.
Soon we'll hear the clarion call.
Jeshua is coming for His Bride.
His pace is fast and wide.
He's calling His own from every Nation.
Watchmen hold steadfast your station.
The call will go out far and wide.
On warrior stallions, we'll ride.
Warrior Brides are we,
Following our King faithfully.
Our armor is proven and true.
The voice of the trump is our cue.
Rise up, Warrior, Rise up!
The time has come to sup.
Specially designed by our King,
He will place on our finger His ring.
Forever in Eternity,
Bound to Him we'll be.
His precious, beautiful Bride,
We'll rule and reign by His side.

## The Warrior Bride

Warrior Bride, Warrior Bride,
Are you ready to ride?
With a sword in hand,
Are you ready to stand?
With praises from your mouth,
Are you ready to shout?
Your shield is His story.
You're clothed with garments of glory.
With the Gospel of Peace on your feet,
Are you ready to protect the wheat?
Hold your horse steady,
With reins in hand, is he ready?
Raise your banners high!
Victory has come nigh!
The battle belongs to the King!
Let the Bridal song ring!
Forward, march on!
The battle has already been won!

# A Ready Bride

The Lord is coming for His Bride!
In crystal chariots we shall ride.
The stallions are ready.
Angels, hold them steady.
To meet the Bridegroom and sup,
They're eager to take us up.
While Angels guard each silver rein,
The Bride tried in fire will not feign.
We are partakers of His story,
With garments made of His glory.
A crown He places upon our head;
For in Him we are led.
We'll cast it at His feet.
Without Him, we'd be beat.
A ring He has for our finger,
Don't pause or linger.
Step ever so lightly into the carriage.
The Bridegroom is ready for this marriage.
"Lord, I'm so excited to meet You!
Oh, how my heart skips a beat or two!
To spend eternity with You,
Is my 'fairytale' come true!"

## The Bridal Crown

A bridal crown for you,
For a Bride whose tried and true.
The jewels we gained on the crown,
Will all soon be thrown down,
At the feet of our Lord,
As we march forward.
Running the race with all our might,
We're an over-comer, dressed in white.
We are sons and daughters of the King,
Sealed with His signet ring.
Our name is written upon a white stone,
We graciously receive it at the throne.
A precious, holy Bride,
Consumed by fire and tried.
A manifestation of His desire,
Is a heart on fire.
"All glory and honor to our King!"
Rejoicing, the Angels sing.
As we humbly lay them down,
His glory shines from the crown.

## He Calls Me Rose

"I call you My Rose,
Whose heart for Me glows.
I want you to see,
You're precious to Me.
The plans I have for you,
You will carry them through.
I will be at your side,
Together we'll ride.
You'll go to the land I love,
There to witness, My turtledove.
Messiah soon will come.
Can you hear the beat of the drum?
The saints are marching to the beat.
I'm coming to gather the wheat.
Angels will trample the tares under their feet,
No more a part of the field of wheat.
The wind of the Spirit will blow away the chaff.
The wheat will bow under My staff.
The banquet table is ready.
On your course, be steady.
The Bride has a special place,
Under My mantle of grace.
The new wine is ready to sip.
A crystal glass awaits the touch of her lip."

# Key to the Kingdom

"A key to the Kingdom I've given to thee.
It'll open the heavens, just wait and see.
I've many things to show you,
And speak to you too.
Just open your eyes,
I have a surprise.
To clearly hear,
Open your ear.
I'll send the Angels to guide you,
And carry you through,
To the heavens above,
Where you'll feel My love.
Get yourself ready.
Remain awake and steady.
It'll be sooner than you think.
Remember My wink?
I've much to tell you, My dear.
I want so much to draw you near.
You have much love for Me.
Come up now and see.
In the vault of blue,
Treasures I have for you.
There are gems galore,
And much more in My store.
Rings for each finger,
With you, I want to linger.
Dressed in a raiment of white,
We'll dance throughout the night.
My Spirit in you dwells,
Your heart for Me so swells.
A passion so strong,
With Me you belong.
On earth you are not satisfied,

For many to you have lied.
You feel so lost in the crowd,
Even though you shout out loud.
They look down upon you as nothing,
That's why I bring You this ring.
You are special like the snowflake,
And sweet as a cream puff cake.
I love you so much!
Come up higher and feel My touch.
Walking down the streets of gold,
There is much that needs to be told."

# The Camels are Coming

The camels are coming, the camels are coming,
I hear a soft strumming.
You can't imagine what's in store.
They're bringing treasures galore.
So, open wide your door,
For there is so much more.
Treasure chests filled with gold,
Revelation will unfold.
Words of wisdom are your tools,
In the chests filled with precious jewels.
They're the keys that unlock,
Each chest as it will dock.
They've traveled the road of understanding,
Now, you're ready for their landing.
You have searched for much knowledge,
I now bring it to your cottage.
As each camel bends its knee,
It gives honor to you, My Bride to be.
The caravan is very long,
Everything I have, My Bride, to you it will belong.
So My dear, hold your head up high,
Your Bridegroom draws nigh!
Fill your heart with anticipation,
Steadfast in your present station.
I've prepared the bridal chamber.
Soon, you'll enter there.
Do not fret and worry,
Or set yourself to scurry.
As you seek Me in the night,
The time will be perfect and right.
I have not forgotten you.
My love remains forever true.
The last will be first,

So, continue to hunger and thirst.
You will be continually fed,
As you partake of My bread.
You are My Temple of Treasure,
Who gives Me great pleasure.

## Little Princess

"My precious Princess, little girl.
Won't you come to dance and twirl?
How I love to see you smile,
As you dance in perfect style.
Your gown, a golden white,
With pink shoes, what a delight!
A crown for one, who is so fair,
I give you roses for your hair.
I give you diamonds for a ring.
Oh, how I love to hear you sing!
Will you then have tea with Me?
We'll traverse across land and sea.
So precious is our time,
Sweet daughter of Mine."

# Heaven's Bride

The Bride patiently waits,
As Angels open heaven's gates.
Our Messiah King is coming soon.
Can you hear the heavenly tune?
The Bride dressed in white,
Oh, what a beautiful sight!
Layers and layers of pure chiffon,
What else will she have on?
Jewels so rare,
They make everyone stare.
A ring upon her finger,
With Him, she loves to linger.
A seal of His love for her,
Oh how it makes her heart stir!
Shoes so ready to dance,
Like the warrior in his stance.
Prancing around, yet so steady,
Jeshua's horse is ready,
Soon the clarion will sound,
And we'll be heaven bound!

Are you ready to leave the ground?

# The Secret Garden

"Come away to My secret place,
There I will speak with you face to face.
I'll tell you of wondrous things,
While the mocking bird sings.
I will woo you like the dove,
And embrace you with all My love.
You are My precious Bride
From whom, nothing will I hide.
My darling, you've captured My heart.
From My arms of love, I'll never let you part.
Lay your head upon My chest.
I will give you perfect rest."

## A Walk in the Garden

Lord, I want to walk in the garden with You,
And sing and dance to a tune or two.
The air is so brisk and clean.
All Your Angels can be seen.
Open my eyes to Your revelation,
As we sit at each station.
The birds and bees fly so free.
That's how You meant it to be.
The colors are so clear and bright.
Your garden is such a beautiful sight.
May I stop to smell a rose?
The fragrance is so stimulating to the nose.
The aroma in the garden is so divine.
It makes me feel like I'm drunk with wine.
The daisies look so pure and white.
Their golden centers are so bright.
The pansies bow their heads to You.
Each and every flower adores You too.
It's an honor to walk with You, my King,
Along the path, while Angels sing.
I love You so, my Lord!
I'm excited to venture forward.
With a wave or a nod to say, "Hi",
The saints of old are passing by.
It's so precious to see them all,
Each one has a special call.
I see the Prophets of old.
I long to hear their stories told.
Many gave up so much for You,
Help me surrender my life too.
The path is made of pure gold,
Each brick has a story to be told.
Gathering things that have no worth,

Our life is so short upon this earth.
Help me to realize,
As I look into Your eyes,
What matters the most,
Is a walk with You as my Host.
The days go by so fast,
Soon, a moment is the past.
Help us to treasure the time with You,
In all the things we say and do.
You gave Your precious life for me,
That I may have eyes to see,
The wonders of each day,
That You send my way.
Whatever trial that comes along,
Help me rise above it with a song.
With You all joy returns,
Oh, how my heart burns.
A purified priestess in Your temple,
One humble and simple.
Let the rain of Your presence fall on me,
Your glory flowing so others may see.
May their eyes be opened to the Truth,
And their life bear much fruit.
The harvest Angels will soon appear.
Many will struggle amidst the fear.
Yet, Your Words will conquer all,
And the enemy will certainly fall.
Lord, if I wander down a different trail,
Pull me inside Your heavenly rail.
The garden path is narrow there.
It's time to climb up the stair.

# The Eagle Soars

"When the thunder roars,
The eagle soars,
High above the mountain tops,
Where the storm stops.
So, spread your wings and soar.
Come up here where there is much more.
You'll leave the earthly domain,
And enter the heavenly plane.
Higher and higher My love, you'll soar,
Until you enter My throne room door.
The door will open wide,
And you'll enter inside.
My love for you I will not hide,
With Me you will abide.
I'll give you spiritual eyes to see,
All I have planned for you to be.
I'll share with you secrets of the Ages,
As I open the Book of many pages.
So My darling, don't fear you're behind.
My destiny for you will soon unwind.
I have much for you to do.
Together, we will walk it through.
Confident that I'll show you the way,
Now, fly through each day."

## Dancing with the Lord

Lord, I long to worship You,
In all I say and do.
With my hands raised high,
I want to touch the sky.
I give honor to You,
For Your heart is true.
As my banners wave about,
From my mouth comes a shout.
"All glory and honor to You belong,"
This is my heart's song.
Like fine horses prancing,
My feet start a dancing.
I love to whirl and twirl,
For I am Your precious pearl.
I want to dance upon the throne room floor,
With You, my Lord, I want to soar.
Soaring to the heights above,
I'm captivated by Your love.
I'd love to waltz upon the crystal floor,
And tango through the throne room door.
I'd like to cha-cha with You by my side,
Along the crystal floor we freely glide.
Then there's the salsa, rumba and mamba.
Wow, with You we're quite a comba!
I love You so my King;
Forever I will sing,
Of Your love and compassion,
To a world that goes a dashin',
Looking for love in all the wrong places,
Running here and there in many races.
We need to stop and smell the roses,

Before life's door closes.
You are the Rose of Sharon,
I hear the trumpets a blaren!

# The Lord's Response

"Oh My precious, beautiful Bride,
With strings of love, to My heart you're tied.
Yes, I will dance with you,
And for all eternity too.
We'll do the tango on the crystal floor,
And I'll show you so much more.
There are heavenly dances that you do not know,
But for you, My Bride, I'm eager to show.
At the banquet table we'll dine,
And drink of the heavenly wine.
I'll gather each Bride alone,
And we'll dance around the heavenly throne.
As I make all things new,
I've much for My Bride to do.
There are Nations to see,
That need to hear of Me.
On My wings of love you'll soar,
As we dance across the floor.
My Father and yours, loves to see us dance,
For it is part of the worship stance.
A dancing warrior I've made you,
Believe Me, it's true!
It's a weapon that makes the devil tremble,
And makes his followers disassemble.
So dance, My beautiful warrior, dance for Me.
The entire world will soon see,
That My mercy is great,
And I will make all things straight.
Stomp your feet,
It brings defeat,
To the enemies plan against you.
I'm stomping there with you too!
I've won the victory,

Let's dance and celebrate My story."
'Oh my Lord, I love to hear Your word.
In my hand it's like a mighty sword.
My dancing boots are on.
Let's dance to the victory You've won!'

# The Cross and a Key

"The Cross is a symbol of My love.
The key is from My Kingdom above.
I unlocked hell's door,
To set captives free and so much more.
Here is the key to My Kingdom,
Where all blessings come from.
The lion's roar,
Opens My door
To a bountiful treasure,
For it gives Me great pleasure.
There are ancient books of stories untold,
Chests filled with jewels, coins, silver and gold.
Secrets that have never been told,
Now will begin to unfold.
My daughter, I love you so much,
Come up and surrender to My touch.
I have much to tell you,
And much for you to do.
You are My Bride tried and true,
Purified by the trials of life and made anew.
With Me you will ride,
Forever at My side,
On wings of love,
We'll soar to the heights above."
"Your treasures are so beautiful to see,
Thank You, my King for this golden key."

## Victory Triumphant

"My beautiful, beautiful Bride,
Let's go for a ride.
My white stallion is steady.
He is saddled and ready.
Would you like your own horse?
Victory Triumphant, of course.
You must get to know him, My dear.
To ride him, you must have no fear.
He'll carry you on through the battle.
You'll ride upon him with no saddle.
He has lightning power,
To scale every tower.
His eyes are like fire,
To match your burning desire.
The battle is so fierce,
The darkness you'll pierce.
With My sword in your hand,
You will take the land.
Victory has many colors, from white to dark.
His hooves carry many a spark.
They'll counterattack every dart,
That Satan throws to try to rip you apart.
Victory has his orders from Me.
Just believe and you'll see.
My dear, now let's go on the ride.
I'm right here by your side.
My precious Warrior Bride,
I'll show you how to ride.
We'll ride on the wind so strong,
Galloping so swiftly along.
His tail and mane flow so free,
On his back you're meant to be.
He's so gentle with you.

Your body moves with him too.
I have a special sword for you,
It'll pierce the darkness through and through.
My glory is your shield.
That's why the enemy will yield.
I have conquered him.
Heaven's realm, now enter in."
'I'm glad to have met Victory,
And be part of his story.
Lord, I know with me You abide.
Thank You for this awesome ride!'

# Sapphires Glowing with the Father's Desire

# Faces over the Water

As El Al approached the Holy Land,
A vision I saw; help me to understand.
I saw many a face over the waters,
Oh Israel, are these your sons and daughters,
Watching and waiting to see
What will be?
They've given their lives for the land.
Will you also take your stand?
You are sojourners there,
God's Covenant must not be broken, none dare!
He promised a land of milk and honey,
It must not be divided for any amount of money.
Come back Israel, come back,
To the true God who shows you no lack.
Your hearts will soon be open,
The scales on your eyes broken.
Messiah's love for you will pour in,
Then you'll repent of your sin.

# Heart Beat of the Father

"Oh Israel, Israel," He whispers in my ear.
"The people and the land are, to Me, dear.
I'm calling them from the North and South,
Salvation and redemption is what it's about.
I'm calling them from the East and West,
To bring them home to forever rest.
Can you hear the pounding of My heart?
Too long from Me you've been apart.
You have been through many a test,
Come Israel, and enter into My rest."

# A Holy Nation

"Oh Israel, I've called you to be a Holy Nation,
One to show every generation.
There is only one God for all Nations to see,
With a pure heart to follow Me.
I've called you to the Desert land.
There I'll show you how to stand.
Lush, green and fragrant to the nose,
I'll make the Desert bloom like a rose.
You're a miracle in the Desert heat,
With fields and fields of bread to eat!
Vegetation, vegetation all around,
Food a plenty will abound.
The best is yet to be,
In Jerusalem, where you'll worship Me!"

## Engraved In the Palm of His Hand

"Oh Israel, Israel,
You are engraved in the palm of My hand.
I have carried you in My arms from Egypt's land.
Remember, I have a Covenant with you,
Through Abraham, Isaac and Jacob, whom I knew.
Rise up and take your stand!
You are only sojourners in My land.
I'm holding you in My lap,
No one shall take you off the map!"

# Israel on the Altar

"I have placed Israel upon My altar,
In My presence, she will not falter.
Amidst the many trials and tears,
I have carried her through the years.
Yet, she wouldn't call upon Me.
Now, it's time for her to see,
Her only 'peace' station,
Is My Rock of salvation".
The land, the land they cry!
Where shall we go, they sigh!
Come back to the God you once knew.
He will carry you through.
You're only sojourners in the land.
Messiah is coming back to take His stand.
His throne was established on Jerusalem of old;
A new City of Gold will now unfold.
Praise and worship all Nations will bring,
To honor and adore, Jeshua, our King!

# Daughter of Zion

"Oh precious Daughter of Zion,
You're from the tribe of Judah, the lion.
Your roar is so strong.
In Beulah land is where you belong.
Come to the land!
There, take your stand.
I'll give you the words to speak.
Fear not, you're not weak.
Tell them My story,
Then, I'll show them My glory.
I love them so much!
Through you, they'll feel My touch.
Garments of glory I've given you to wear,
As My faithful Ambassador there.
Be obedient to My voice.
Make it your ultimate choice.
On wings of prayer in the sky,
To Israel you will fly."

# Longing for Jerusalem

Lord, I long for the hills of Jerusalem,
The land You were born in.
Oh, to walk along the Galilee,
Strolling along, just You and me.
Tell me about the time You were here.
I can't help but shed a tear.
You love Your people so much.
Open their eyes with Your tender touch.
Reflected on the footprints in the sand,
I see Your glory throughout this land.
I want to walk the land with You,
Like the Patriots of old were called to do.
Your presence in the land is so strong.
I know that this is where I belong.

# Jerusalem Hills

In the Jerusalem hills His name is written,
Where His people have been totally smitten.
For years they traversed their own way.
From His shelter, they chose to stray.
"It's time for them to return!"
His voice is bold and stern.
"My love for them is so strong,
Under My Sukkah is where they belong.
Soon, I'll rip the veil from their eyes,
When I hear their heart cries.
They will know that I AM their God,
As they tremble at Calvary's rod.
Soon My Son in the cloud will appear,
The Nations will know that judgment is near.
When Jeshua steps upon the mountain,
A river will pour forth like a fountain.
The earth will tremble and quake;
The hearts of creation will break.
Comfort, comfort My people now.
Wipe every tear from their brow.
Soon I am coming.
Do you not hear the drums a drumming?
Arise My Warriors, arise,
To the sound of My people's cries.
For the soon coming day,
Prepare the way, Prepare the way!
I'm coming upon a white horse,
To change history's course.
I have given them the Covenant land,
Warriors on this you must stand.
Pray, Pray, Pray,

On this and every day,
For peace to come to this land,
For in these hills I have My brand."

# Oh Israel

"Oh Israel, Israel can you not see,
I have placed My face as a flint toward thee.
For you to tell all Nations My story,
Around you, I've placed My glory.
With each trial and test,
I've held you close to My chest.
Yet, you rebelled.
To other gods you were compelled.
As a mother holds her babe to breast,
Come back to Me, I'll give you rest.
I will uplift you,
And fill you with the morning dew.
The Nations are gathering around you,
But My Word remains true.
I have written My name in Jerusalem's mountains.
Out of her belly will burst many fountains.
The water will flow so sweet and pure,
To all Nations it will be a lure.
I love you with an everlasting love,
That flows from the Father above.
Return to Me, and you will see,
How the mighty Hand of God will set you free!"

# Elijah's Cup

Elijah's cup, Elijah's cup!
My dear Lord, what's up?
"Look deep within the brim.
Can you not see Elijah in the trim?
He is wearing a garment of praise,
Standing with arms upraised.
He is calling all who will listen.
Only pure hearts like gold will glisten.
The Bride will not tarry,
Under the mantle he will carry.
He is standing on the Torah Scroll.
The truth to Israel will now unroll.
Over him is a chuppah of lilies so pure;
Hardened hearts the scent will lure.
As the heavenly harps are playing,
Those who don't respond are staying.
Just before the great attack,
The fiery chariot is coming back."
Lift up your eyes to the heavenly blue.
The Lord is returning, believe, it is true!

# Return Oh Israel

"Oh Israel, Israel, time is running out.
Do you hear My clarion shout?
I have you in the palm of My hand.
There has been so much fighting in My land.
Come back and honor Me!
Miracles in the land you'll see.
To take the Torah to the world to be shown,
Is why I called you to be My very own.
It's time for Ephraim to come home;
Judah must not fight alone.
Under the Banner of the Lord,
You will be joined in one accord."

# Deborah, the Bee

Deborah, Deborah, what a bee!
A mighty warrior was she!
As bold as a lion,
When Israel came a cryin'.
With the Lord as her shield,
Bravely, she went into the field.
"Arise, Deborah, arise!
Enter into My surprise.
I will give you Nations as your spoil,
For all your obedient toil.
With the sting of the hornet,
I'll send My coronet.
It'll pierce every heart,
And counter every dart,
To cause you to bend or sway,
That Satan tries to send your way.
I have made you steadfast,
With strength and stamina to last.
Put on your garment of worship and praise,
Victory comes with arms upraised."

# New Wine

Oh Israel, Israel, you are His precious flower.
The name of the Lord is your strong tower.
Your petals have been pressed,
Through years of hunger, you became stressed.
It's time to come back to the Lord,
For He is your perfect reward.
Miracles and healings you will see,
As the people and land are set free.
He loves you with an everlasting love;
A Covenant sealed with the Father above.
Arise, oh Jerusalem and shine.
Come and drink of the new wine!

## Lion of Judah Roar

Oh Lion of Judah roar,
While the eagles soar!
"My people come back to My land,
There with your brothers, take a stand!
It's time for Ephraim
And Judah to join again.
You have been separated too long.
United together with Me you belong.
Judah, lay down your pride,
Ephraim, cast off your sin, don't hide.
Joined together in one song,
This is where you belong.
I am the Vine, you are the branches,
There won't be many more chances.
Raise up high your banner.
Hear the Prophets' stammer:
'Return to Me, Return to Me,'
A miraculous healing you'll see!"

# The Call of I AM

"Oh Israel, Israel, do you understand?
They'll not drive you out of My land.
My Covenant with Abraham, Isaac and Jacob, I stand.
I have given you this Promised Land.
A Holy Nation for Me,
I've called you to be.
You've wandered a far,
And followed your own star.
I AM that I AM calls you again.
Repent of your rebellious sin.
I've carried you on My wings,
Yet you sought after worldly things.
Return to Me and you'll see,
The miracles that will come to be.
Jeshua, the Word, came to you first.
For Him you didn't hunger or thirst.
The Gentile Nations sought after Him,
Now it's time for you to come in.
My arms are opened wide,
Beckoning you to come inside.
The veil from your eyes will soon lift,
Then you'll understand and not drift.
I'm calling Ephraim back to the land.
There with Judah to take their rightful stand.
Never to bow to another thing,
Will you stand with Jerusalem's King?"

# The Burning Bush

When Moses saw the bush on fire,
He went closer to inquire.
"You're standing on Holy ground,"
From the bush came the sound.
"Take off your shoes,
For you I choose,
To set My people free,
From Egypt to liberty.
Bow down and worship Me.
Great and mighty things you'll see.
With your staff, go back to the land.
There with Aaron, take a stand.
At My command,
The people are to leave the land.
They'll traverse the desert hot,
Until they reach my appointed spot,
A land flowing with milk and honey,
With golden glory, oh so sunny.
So, forward, march on,
The victory has already been won!"

# Scattered Pearls

## Virtuous Women

Virtuous women are we,
For we belong to God's family.
Filled with Truth from His Word,
Boldly, we move forward.
Carrying the Word in our hand,
We go throughout the land.
With a mantle of compassion,
It's our garment of fashion.
To serve and carry our love to any length,
We're girded with dignity and strength.
Our hands extend to the poor,
Holding nothing back, we're more than a doer.
With our hands constantly open,
We release healing to hearts that are broken.
Wisdom flows freely from our mouth,
Speaking softly, words of kindness all about.
Idleness is not part of our name,
And covertness is not our gain.
Rising early in the night,
We seek Your guiding light.
Bless our families and every friend,
Grant peace and joy to never end.
On our knees we humbly pray,
Help us this day,
To be the women you destined us for,
Like a fountain, pouring out blessings and much more.
Lord, may we always give You pleasure,
And be Your precious treasure.

## Stepping Stones to Problem Solving

To understand a problem, one must act.
First, gather each and every fact.
Then, listen with your heart and head,
To each and every word that's said.
Tell me what happened here.
Was something not made clear?
Are these the facts you meant?
The message to the head is now sent.
Next, identify the cause.
Stop, listen and pause.
What action took place, I say?
Instead, it should have been this way.
I see the problem that went wrong.
Good service truly is our song.
Let's discuss each resolution,
And come up with a good conclusion.
To maintain a good customer relation,
We aim to solve the situation.
We aim to please, is our motto.
A big smile on your face, a lasting photo!

# Teamwork

Teamwork, teamwork let's all shout!
Let me tell you what it's about.
This is how it should start.
Each member has a vital part.
Like a circle never ending,
Hearts and spirits joined, never bending.
Cooperation is the game.
A life shared is never the same.
Toting the load together,
Makes it feel like a feather.
Reaching out to play our role,
United together, we reach our goal!

# Life's Pathway

As you walk along life's path,
This is the crossroad we meet at.
First a smile, then a greeting,
To everyone you are meeting.
Value each person as a precious pearl.
It will fill your heart with joy to swirl.
"How may I help you?" You ask.
Listen to their response, take off your mask.
Help them with their wants and needs,
For we are here to perform such deeds.
I'm grateful for the honor to have met you.
Hope to see you soon again, too!

# Sisters by Heart

A sister in the natural, I do not have.
A sister in the spirit is like healing salve.
When life takes its toll,
She brings sunshine to my soul.
When my soul cries,
And tears fill my eyes,
Hers twinkle with hope,
And she helps me to cope.
When the road is rough,
And the walk is tough,
She extends a hand,
And helps me to stand.
When my heart is broken,
An encouraging word is spoken.
Nothing can compare
To a heart filled with care.
My sister by heart, I adopt you,
Will you adopt me too?

## Lady Bug

Lady Bug, Lady Bug what's under your shell?
Is it your life story, pray tell?
The spots on your back,
Shows you have no lack.
The shell with a color of red,
In your life, much is to be said.
You dance upon the green leaves,
Your life story, it weaves.
So strikingly created by the Divine,
Oh Lady Bug, Lady Bug, you are so fine.
Lady Bug, Lady Bug dance to the tune,
Your Master, the King is coming soon!

# Friendship

A friend is one, who's always there,
Through thick and thin, they always care.
When you fall,
They hear your call.
They extend a helping hand
To help you stand.
Someone to share a dream with;
They won't criticize you for it.
They hold your secrets deep within,
And don't spread them on a whim.
They are there to pray,
And encourage you on the way.
They share laughter and sorrow,
They bring hope for tomorrow.
No matter the distance or years,
Precious memories erase the tears.
I thank God, for you, my friend.
Much love and blessings to you I send.

# Our Flower Shop

Here's to our flower shop to be.
We'll make it beautiful for all to see.
There will be Roses galore,
Scattered throughout the store.
Let's add a Cyclamen or two,
With Forget-Me-Nots in blue.
We will not be lazy,
So we'll throw in a Daisy.
We must have Sunflowers too,
To bring a smile or two.
Let's not forget the Fichus trees,
Snapdragons and Sweet Peas.
How about a Calla Lily so pure and white?
Wouldn't that be a beautiful sight?
Let's have fun and be silly,
And add many a Tiger Lily.
As customers come through the door,
Soon, we'll hear the roar.
For those who want an exotic flair,
We'll scatter Orchids everywhere.
Oh, let's not forget the Carnations,
Different colors around the stations.
On a black velvet display,
We'll have a jewelry array.
They will add sparkle in the store,
To lure people through the door.
How about a homemade card or two?
Wouldn't it be nice for our dream to come true?

## Thank Goodness it's Friday!

"Wow!" The week went by so fast.
Thank Goodness, it's Friday at last.
Now, when the sun goes down,
Put on a smile and paint the town.
On Saturday, it's time to do the chores.
How about baking a pan of s'mores?
When the day is done,
Go ahead have some fun.
Sunday, a day of worship, so look your best,
And be sure you get a lot of rest.
When the sun next arises,
You'll face Monday's surprises!

## Printer Failure

What do you do when the printer goes down?
Well, you start with a frown.
Then you end up on your knees.
Trouble shooting isn't always a breeze.
Touch this key, touch that key,
Oh my, what could it be?
I'll put on a smile,
And turn it off for awhile.
When I turn it on, it begins to work.
Then, another quirk.
Back to square one,
This isn't much fun.
Soon, after many a try,
The pages start to fly.
The Doctor gave a grateful shout!
I was happy that I could help him out.

I dedicate this poem to Dr. P. Nakazato

# The Lady of Passion

Dear lady of fashion,
Wearing a mantle of passion,
Who is your lover to be?
Shall we just wait and see?
Is it the hot Italian,
As free as a wild stallion?
Or the man on the plane,
With a Hebraic name?
Enter now, the man of God so deep.
Is he the one for you to keep?
There are so many more,
That open passion's door.
How does her heart choose?
Love burns to all, none she wants to lose.
A vessel of love,
Formed from above,
With an eternal flame
To carry His name.
A passion that burns so bright,
Like a candle in the night.
Hearts in sync,
Pondering every wink,
Intense as the desert heat,
She's swiftly carried off her feet.
A channel of love,
Flowing from above.
A light to light the way,
To those who tend to stray.
Who shall carry this awesome passion?
One who has been given much compassion.
Who will capture her heart?
The one who remains faithful from the start!

# The Surgeon

A surgeon's work is never done,
From one case to another, he must run.
A stitch here, and a stitch there,
You know he does care.
A case may take long,
He doesn't want it to go wrong.
He will check the procedure twice,
For, everything must be precise.
His hands are gentle like a dove,
Carefully dissecting with his glove.
Compassion is his virtue,
To his patient he remains true.
As the captain of the team,
He will not yell or scream.
Patiently receiving every call,
He's considerate of all.
When the case is finished,
Patient care is not diminished.
Making sure all is well, when the case is done,
Only then will he start another one.
Doctor, thank you for all you do,
And may God bless you too!

I dedicate this to the surgeons I work with.

# The Joys of Charge in the OR

Working at the Core desk is certainly not a bore.
I ponder the board to see what's in store.
Are the cases on time?
Or are they all in a line?
Will I have enough staff?
Shall I sigh or laugh?
I walk around to check each room.
Will the case be long or end soon?
I need to know because of staff,
The Docs continue on, sometimes with a laugh.
Back to the desk I go,
Updating the board with what I know.
Then the phones begin to ring.
What are the words they bring?
The offices close, the Docs are ready to do their case.
Can you speed up the OR pace?
Will my case be on time?
Or am I pushed back to nine?
Can you move my case?
Why not mix the strips, and change my place,
Or throw the strips up in the air?
You had a case? Now, it's not there!
Sorry, Doc, I can't do that,
But this is where it's at.
You see Doc, you'll have to wait.
The case ahead is running late.
As soon as they start a closin'
You're the next chosen.
Now it's time for the change of shift.
Will I have enough staff, get my drift?
The phone continues to ring,
Someone always wants some thing.
Then I hear a voice down the hall,

I need the Doc, can you call?
Now it's time to spread Room Eleven,
Then, please open Room Seven.
Please turn over Room Eight,
The case must not be late.
The next case will go in Room Three,
I need you to spread it, you're free.
Is it time for you to go?
Well, this I want you to know.
You've done a great job in this place,
You've kept up with the pace.
Working in the OR can be fun.
It sure keeps you on the run.
When the day does end,
You must catch a fresh wind.
For tomorrow will soon arrive,
And once again, the strips come alive!


I dedicate this poem to Dr. H. Comstock

# A Trip to the Mall

Oh honey, you're not getting older.
Consider it just a lot more, bolder.
Why look, you still have those rollers in your hair,
And you don't care if people stare.
These glasses help us to see,
The sales, and what AARP says is free.
Why dear, there's still a spring in your step.
All those vitamins give you pep.
We still can carry a big shopping bag,
Even though our paces drag.
Open that paper in your hand,
And let's march to the shopping band.
Just think, we're getting an early start,
To the "blue light" special at K-Mart.
We can grab a cart,
Then, run to the new Wal-Mart.
We definitely have to hit Park Mall.
There we'll have a ball!
There are so many stores to choose from.
Won't it be a lot of fun?
Are you ready for a noon break?
How about some cheese cake?
People are so attentive with care.
It must be the rollers in your hair.
Oh, this is so much fun,
But we have to be on the run.
Time is flying by so fast,
We must make this day last.
We have to hit every store.
My shopping bag needs a little more.
My purse seems to be a little lighter,
But, my spirits are much brighter.
Well, my friend,

This day has come to an end.
Hope you had as much fun as I did.
It reminds me of when I was a kid.

## Heart Cries

Lord, what is the purpose of creation?
There are so many hurting hearts around the Nation.
The young generation is crying for help,
Like the sound of a young lion's yelp.
Who will alleviate their pain?
What will remain?
The cry is getting stronger.
Can we bear it much longer?
Who will arise to the call,
To lift those up who fall?
The burden is so heavy.
Soon it will burst the gates of the levy.
"Prayer warriors arise.
You must not compromise.
You must stand in the gap,
And drink of My sap.
I have given you the power.
So, rise up in faith this hour.
The floodgates are open,
All is not broken.
Let the waters wash over the pain.
Warriors, My Word it will contain.
The healing will flow.
Grace and mercy I bestow.
Lift your eyes up to the hill,
Your spirit, My love will fill.
Praise My Holy Name.
I am always the same.
Cast your burden upon Me.
Miracles of suddenly you'll see.
Hearts are mended in My rain.
Souls will never be the same.
Praise and worship every day,

Brings My intimacy in to stay.
Why worry about tomorrow?
It only brings much sorrow.
My wings will shelter you,
Just let My Spirit flow through.
Be at peace, as you go on your way.
This is My Word for today."

# The Prophet

The Prophet has a lonely walk,
It makes many turn and balk.
They do not understand,
A Prophet has to take a stand.
Through rain, heat and snow,
In obedience they must go.
In supplication and prayer,
They are the Lord's wayfarer.
With no place to lay their head,
They must venture on ahead.
The Word is their meat,
And torn sandals upon their feet.
A staff secure in their hand,
With each step they traverse the land.
Their garments are well worn,
And their hearts, totally shorn.
They are called of the Lord,
And not by man's board.
To a World definitely amiss,
They are called as a witness.
Their message is to repent,
Before the end time event.
Their message is loud and clear,
So all will hear.
"To God, you must return,"
With a voice that's stern.

## Destination Excellence

Sometimes we wonder if the work we've done,
Has a bearing on anyone.
Solving problems that come our way,
We put in many hours a day.
Then an idea comes to mind;
To keep costs down, we must find.
We develop a plan or two,
And work to carry it through.
We gather the results,
And work out the ins and outs.
The plan is ready to submit.
Soon it becomes a hit.
To Destination Excellence every day,
Cost containment is the way.

# I Ponder the Snow

As I ponder the snow falling today,
I see each snowflake, a treasure on the way.
As it floats down from the sky,
I examine it carefully with my eye.
Such intricate detail of heavenly lace,
As it falls to it's designated place.
Each one, a royal pattern from the King,
Father, what message does it bring?
"In a world unable to cope,
They bring a message of hope.
My message is simple and pure,
In Me, they will be secure.
Each one represents a soul,
That I long to make completely whole.
As the snow blankets the earth,
It brings a revelation of new birth.
The blanket of snow is so pure and white,
Like a regenerated soul in My sight.
When the rays of the Son shine upon it,
Facets of beautiful diamonds are lit."

# The Oasis of His Love

Bubbling pools of water: Refreshment IS. 28:11-12
Healing springs from the Father: IS. 49:10
The palm tree stands so tall: PS. 92:15
Roots deep in the ground: Grounded in Him:
-LOVE- EP. 3:17, PR. 12:12
A place of shade: PS. 121:5 Rest in His presence.
The effulgence of His glory so bright: EZ. 10:4
The heat of His presence brings healing: IS. 6:6-7
Fanning with the palm branches can't diminish the flames
within.
An unquenchable thirst for Him: MAT. 5:6: JN. 6:35
The fruit, dates, sweet to the lips,
His spoken Words: PR. 11:30

**THE RIGHTEOUS SHALL FLOURISH**
**LIKE A PALM TREE**
**PS. 92:12**

# Peace and Blessings!

CPSIA information can be obtained at www.ICGtesting.com
Printed in the USA
BVOW070657221111

276633BV00002B/4/P